POWER THOUGHTS

Stimulate Your Creativity
and Develop Great Thoughts
with Priceless Quotes

Samson Olusanya King

To all those men and women who have encouraged, inspired, and motivated me over the years, and continues to do so. Your impacts on my life, family, and the world are invaluable. This is another one for you!

CONTENTS

INTRODUCTION

Can you imagine for a second that you were alive hundreds of years ago, and you desired to meet or have lunch with some of the world's greatest thinkers and hear their thoughts? I can guarantee that pulling such a feat off will cost even the filthy rich person a fortune – traveling around the globe, locating those men and women, and having life-changing conversations with them. Not only will it be crazily expensive, but it might take you your whole lifetime to accomplish. Thanks to technology that has made it possible for almost everyone to have access to the thoughts of many of the world's greatest thinkers in any area of human endeavors.

My passion for quote collection dates to my high school years. I grew up with my grandmother who did not have the opportunity of stepping into the four walls of a classroom to learn literacy (the ability to read and write) but was highly educated when it comes to what we call informal education. I used to think that people who go to traditional schools (elementary, middle school, high school, college, universities, etc.) are the educated ones until I took a Philosophy of Education course and discovered the distinction between literacy and education. I found out that you can go to all the schools you want, get all the degrees and still be ill-educated, uneducated, or miseducated. That is a discussion for another time.

The people in my grandmother's generation speak only the native language of the particular people group they belong to, and my people group from the part of Nigeria I'm from speaks Yoruba. The advent of Westernization introduces English as the official language of the country and learning to write and speak the same became an uphill and arduous task for some of us. I was able to master the art of writing and understanding the English language during my elementary and middle school years to a great extent, but it was very problematic for me to speak. I told my friends that I went to an elementary school where my teacher used Yoruba to teach us English!

Even though my mom and grandma could not read, write, or speak English, they both inspired me to read books. I remember my grandmother mandating that I write letters to my parents in the English language and mail them. While reading books that are written in English, striking statements, sayings, quotes, expressions, etc. caught my attention. I began to write them down and read them repeatedly. The more I did that, the more books I want to read, and I started noticing a positive change in my desire to learn and speak English and grow my thoughts. Growing up with no computer or computer skills, no internet, or other means of storing relevant information, I kept writing the quotes from some of my favorite writers and thinkers in any available notebook.

This book is a collection of eclectic assortments that represents wise sayings, golden nuggets, and musings of the numerous venerable sages. Some of those individuals are still alive here on earth, while others have ceased to be here in the human form, yet millions all over the world continue to be impacted by their thoughts and materials.

This compendium of quotes selected is useful for pepping up speeches, letters, presentations, or just for daily motivation for living. It is the sequel to my book, In the Company of the Greats. Motivation and inspiration don't come naturally to people and Benjamin Disraeli once said, "Nurture your mind with great thoughts. To believe in the heroic makes heroes."

Some may think we do not need quotes from older generations today, but I think they forget that our world never really changes. The fears, challenges, struggles, and anxieties of humans remain the same from generation to generation. We need to know that previous generations had similar struggles, joys, and experiences. You and I must never come to that level that we think we cannot learn from generations before us, and from people in our generation that have encountered unique experiences that can inspire us.

I attempted to correctly attribute each quote to the original author, but in some cases, it was practically impossible to identify such originality. In such a situation whereby the originality of the quote could not be clarified, I attributed the term "unknown". Hopefully, some of my readers will provide the names of such great minds for future references. Above all, I gave credit and honor to whom honor is due.

These quotes are prepared to be of practical service to the reader. I hope that they will inspire, motivate, serve as a tool to stimulate the mind creatively, bring a lot of wonders to your heart and soul, and become an instrument for developing great thoughts.

With My Best
Samson Olusanya King

POWER THOUGTHS COLLECTION

"I have decided to stick with love. Hate
is too great a burden to bear."
- Martin Luther King

"If we could read the secret history of our
enemies, we should find in each man's life sorrow
and suffering enough to disarm all hostility."
- Henry Wadsworth Longfellow

"When life knocks you down, if you
can look up, you can get up."
- Les Brown

"Remember that failure is an event, not a person."
- Zig Ziglar

"Courage is going from failure to failure
without losing your enthusiasm."
- Winston Churchill

"It's what we all wanted when we were children-
to be loved and accepted exactly as we were then,
not when we got taller or thinner or prettier...and
we still want it...but we aren't going to get it from
other people until we can get it from ourselves."
- Louise Hay

"Too many talented people string and
unstring their instruments without
ever playing their music."

- Zig Ziglar

"You don't get to choose how you're
going to die. Or when. But you can decide
how you're going to live now."
- Joan Baez

"The truth is incontrovertible."
- Winston Churchill

"Don't speak unless you can improve
upon the silence."
- Quaker Proverb

"Happiness is not found in things you possess,
but in what you have the courage to release."
- Nathaniel Hawthorne

"Why waking up stressing? When waking
up is a blessing."
- Unknown

"It isn't what you have or who you are or
what you are doing that makes you happy or
unhappy. It is what you think about it."
- Dale Carnegie

"Perfectionism is not the path that
leads us to our gifts and to our sense of
purpose; it's the hazardous detour."

- Brene Brown

"When a man is wrapped up in himself,
he makes a pretty small package."
- John Ruskin

"The greater danger for most of us is not
that our aim is too high and we miss it, but
that it is too low and we reach it."
- Michelangelo

"Nurture great thoughts for you will
never go higher than your thoughts."
- Benjamin Disraeli

"There are a lot of things you can do with
sand, but do not try building a house on it."
- C.S. Lewis

"Do not judge by appearance; a *rich
heart* may be under a *poor coat*."
- Scottish Proverb

"Truth is heavy, so few men carry it."
- Jewish Proverb

"We should never finish a 20-
year program in two years."
- Jack Ma

"When "I" is replaced by "we", even illness
becomes wellness."
- Unknown

"The first duty of love is to listen."
- Paul Tillich

"Fail your way to success."
- Les Brown

"Success is to be measured not so much
by the position that one has reached
in life as by the obstacles which he has
overcome while trying to succeed."
- Booker T. Washington

"The journey of a thousand miles
begins with one step."
- Lao-Tzu

"Whatever we plant in our subconscious
mind and nourish with repetition and
emotion will one day become a reality."
- Earl Nightingale

"Life is like riding a bicycle. To keep your
balance, you must keep moving."
- Albert Einstein

"Words are, of course, the most powerful
drug used by mankind. We have 40 million
reasons for failure, but not a single excuse."
- Rudyard Kipling

"Live life when you have it. Life is a splendid
gift-there is nothing small about it."
- Florence Nightingale

"Brave people don't let failure define
them; they let failure teach them."
- Annie F. Downs

"Failure will never overtake me if my
determination to succeed is strong enough."
- Og Mandino

"Nothing can resist the will of a people."
- Benjamin Disraeli

"In love, the paradox occurs that two
beings become one and yet remain two."
- Erich Fromm

"Certain things catch your eyes but pursue
only those that capture the heart."
- Ancient Indian Proverb

"We must accept finite disappointment,

but we must never lose infinite hope."
- Martin Luther King

"Be intelligently ignorant that you
don't know what you couldn't do."
- Anonymous

"The greatest glory in living lies not in never
failing, but in rising every time we fail."
- Nelson Mandela

"There is more to life than increasing its speed."
- Mahatma Gandhi

"Every man of courage is a man of his word."
- Pierre Corneille

"All life is an experiment. The more
experiments you make the better."
- Ralph Waldo Emerson

"The greatest day in your life and mine is
when we take total responsibility for our
attitudes. That's the day we truly grow up."
- John C. Maxwell

"We can easily forgive a child who is
afraid of the dark; the real tragedy of life
is when men are afraid of the light."
- Plato

"Attitude is a boomerang: Whatever you
throw out there will come back your way."
- John Cena

"Only the dead have seen the end of war."
- Plato

"People are just about as happy as
they make up their minds to be."
- Abraham Lincoln

"You must give time to your fellow men-
even if it's a little thing, do something for
others-something for which you get no
pay but the privilege of doing it."
- Albert Schweitzer

"In the end, it's not the years in your life
that count. It's the life in your years."
- Abraham Lincoln

"There are two ways to be fooled. One
is to believe what isn't true; the other is
to refuse to believe what is true."
- Søren Kierkegaard

"We need four hugs a day for survival. We
need eight hugs a day for maintenance. We
need twelve hugs a day for growth."

- Virginia Satir

"Being ignorant is not so much a shame,
as being unwilling to learn."
- Benjamin Franklin

"Five percent of the people think; ten percent
of the people think they think; and the other
eighty-five percent would rather die than think."
- Thomas A. Edison

"We are all born ignorant, but one must
work hard to remain stupid."
- Benjamin Franklin

"Obstacles cannot crush me. Every obstacle
yields to stern resolve. He who is fixed to
a star does not change his mind."
- Leonardo Da Vinci

"When everything seems to be going
against you, remember that the airplane
takes off against the wind, not with it."
- Henry Ford

"…let me never be afraid of endings or beginnings.
Teach me to embrace all of life with joy."
- Helen Lesman

"Never give up on something that you

can't go a day without thinking about."
- Winston Churchill

"Success is not final; failure is not fatal: it
is the courage to continue that counts."
- Winston Churchill

"It's not the load that weighs you
down, it's how you carry it."
- C.S. Lewis

"I do not think much of a man who is not
wiser today than he was yesterday."
- Abraham Lincoln

"Worry is a small trickle of fear that meanders
through the mind until it cuts a channel into
which all other thoughts are drained."
- Robert Albert Bloch

"If you keep on talking, you will eventually
say something funny."
- Groucho Marx

"An ounce of Mother is worth a bucket of clergy."
- Thomas Sydenham

"Worry is putting a question marks
where God has put periods."
- John Rice

"We can easily manage if we will only take, each day, the burden appointed to it. But the load will be too heavy for us if we carry yesterday's burden over again today, and then add the burden of the morrow before we are required to bear it."
- John Newton

"Present mirth hath present laughter."
- William Shakespeare

"Nothing in life is achieved without effort, daring to take risks, and often some suffering."
- Erich Fromm

"That's one small step for man, one giant leap for mankind."
- Neil Armstrong

"Intellectual integrity, courage, and kindness are still the virtues I admire most."
- Gerti Cori

"...courage and intelligence are the two qualifications best worth a good man's cultivation..."
– Robert Louis Stevenson

"Daring as it is to investigate the unknown, even more so is it to question the known."
- Kaspar

"All our dreams can come true – if we
have the courage to pursue them."
– Walt Disney

"The world is made of stories, not atoms."
- Muriel Rukeyser

"We ought to respect the effect we have on others.
We know by our own experience how much others
affect our lives, and we must remember that we,
in turn, must have the same effect on others."
- George Eliot

"God created *human* because He loves stories."
- Elie Wiesel (Emphasis Mine)

"The greatest power that a person possesses
is the power to choose."
- J. Martin Kohe

"The only limit to our realization of tomorrow
will be our doubts of today. Let us move
forward with strong and active faith."
- Franklin D. Roosevelt

"We increase whatever we praise. The whole
creation responds to praise and is glad."
- Charles Fillmore

"Men go abroad to wonder at the heights of
mountains, at the huge waves of the sea, at the
long courses of the rivers, at the vast compass of
the ocean, at the circular motions of the stars; and
they pass by themselves without wondering."
- St. Augustine

"From quiet homes and first beginning; Out to the
undiscovered ends, There's nothing worth the wear
of winning, but laughter and the love of friends."
- Hilaire Belloc

"Many seek advice, few profits from it."
- Publius Syrus

"Ideal teachers are those who use themselves
as bridges over which they invite their
students to cross, then having facilitated
their crossing, joyfully collapse, encouraging
them to create bridges of their own."
- Leo Buscaglia

"He who has a *why* to live can bear
with almost any *how*."
- Nietzsche

"Heroism…is endurance for one moment more."
- George Kennan

"All I have seen teaches me to trust the
Creator for all I have not seen."
- Ralph Waldo Emerson

"Death is a challenge. It tells us not to
waste time…It tells us to tell each other
right now that we love each other."
- Leo Buscaglia

"Never tell a young person that something
cannot be done. God may have been waiting
for countless centuries for somebody ignorant
enough of the impossibility to do that thing."
- Unknown

"Cherish your visions and your dreams
as they are the children of your soul; the
blueprints of your ultimate achievements."
- Napoleon Hill

"No matter how busy you may think you are,
you must find time for reading, or surrender
yourself to self-chosen ignorance."
- Atwood H. Townsend

"Miss a meal if you have to, but don't miss a book."
- Jim Rohn

"The empires of the future are

the empires of the mind."
- Sir Winston Churchill

"If you want your children to be intelligent,
read them fairy tales. If you want them to be
more intelligent, read them more fairy tales."
- D Albert Einstein

"There are only two ways to live your life.
One is as though nothing is a miracle. The
other is as though everything is a miracle."
- Albert Einstein

"The things that count the most are those things
that cannot be counted-time with family."
- Unknown

"Give your entire attention to what God
is doing right now, and don't get worked up
about what may or may not happen tomorrow.
God will help you deal with whatever hard
things come up when the time comes."
- Matthew 6:34 (*MSG*)

"Impossible is a word to be found
only in the dictionary of fools!"
- Napoleon Bonaparte

"Just because someone is married with
kids doesn't mean they are not lonely. Your

relationship with your spouse can get neglected
in the everyday crush of life's responsibilities.
Make time…the world can wait."
- Lauren Casper

"Make it a rule never to give a child a
book you would not read yourself."
- George Bernard Shaw

"A childhood without books, that would
be no childhood. That would be like being
shut out from the enchanted place where you
can go and find the rarest kind of joy."
- Astrid Lindgren

"Once you learn to read, you will be forever free."
- Frederick Douglass

"There is more treasure in books than in
all the pirate's loot on Treasure Island."
- Walt Disney

"The things I want to know are in
books. My best friend is the man who'll
get me a book I [haven't] read."
- Abraham Lincoln

"The more that you read, the more
things you will know. The more you
learn, the more places you'll go."

- Dr. Seuss

"Any book that helps a child to form a habit
of reading, to make reading one of his deep
and continuing needs, is good for him."
- Maya Angelou

"Books are the bees which carry the quickening
pollen from one to another mind."
- James Russell Lowell

"Rejection is divine protection from a sad future."
- Mike Murdock

"My alma mater was books, a good library ...
I could spend the rest of my life reading,
just satisfying my curiosity."
- Malcolm X

"Some women have a weakness for shoes. I can go
barefoot if necessary. I have a weakness for books."
- Oprah Winfrey

"Though I am grateful for the blessings of wealth,
it hasn't changed who I am. My feet are still on
the ground. I'm just wearing better shoes."
- Oprah Winfrey

"The home should be to the children the most
attractive place in the world, and the mother's

presence should be the greatest attraction."
- Ellen G. White

"Failure is simply the opportunity to begin
again, this time more intelligently."
- Henry Ford

"The greatest mistake you can make in life is to
be continually fearing that you will make one."
- Elbert Hubbard

"If you worry about who is going to get
credit, you don't get much work done."
- Dorothy Height

"Life is a sweeter, stronger, fuller, more gracious
thing for the friend's existence, whether he be
near or far. If the friend is close at hand, that
is best; but if he is far away, he is still there to
think of, to wonder about, to hear from, to
write to, to share life and experience with,
to serve, to honor, to admire, to love."
- Arthur Christopher Benson

"One furnace melts all hearts-love; One balm
soothes all pain-patience; One medicine cures all
ills-time; One light illumines all darkness-hope."
- Ivan Panin

"Beginning today, treat everyone you meet as if

they were going to be dead by midnight. Extend
to them all the care, kindness, and understanding
you can muster, and do it with no thought of any
reward. Your life will never be the same again."
- Og Mandino

"A gentleman is one who puts more
into the world than he takes out."
- George Bernard Shaw

"Take care of your body. It's the
only place you have to live."
- Jim Rohn

"There is no elevator to success;
you have to take the stairs."
- Traditional, *Popularized by Zig Ziglar*

"He has achieved success who has worked
well, laughed often, and loved much."
- Elbert Hubbard

"With the fearful strain that is on me night
and day, if I did not laugh, I should die."
- Abraham Lincoln

"If one advances confidently in the direction
of his dreams, and endeavors to live the
life he has imagined, he will meet with a
success unexpected in common hours."

- Henry David Thoreau

"The doorstep to the temple of wisdom is
the knowledge of our own ignorance."
- Charles H. Spurgeon

"We have done so much, for so long, with so little,
we are now qualified to do anything with nothing."
- Mother Teresa

"Be thankful for what you have; you'll end up
having more. If you concentrate on what you
don't have, you will never, ever have enough."
- Oprah Winfrey

"Optimism is the biology of hope."
- Denis Whitley

"Turn your wounds into wisdom."
- Oprah Winfrey

"When it comes to enthusiasm, be
like a pilot light - Never go out."
- Unknown

"It is when we all play safe that we create
a world of utmost insecurity."
- Dag Hammarskjold

"Nothing great was ever achieved

without enthusiasm."
- Ralph Waldo Emerson

"You are never too old to set another
goal or dream another dream."
- Les Brown

"Most of the important things in the world have
been accomplished by people who have kept on
trying when there seemed to be no hope at all."
- Dale Carnegie

"There's always room for improvement.
It's the biggest room in the house."
- Louise Leber

"Your time is limited, so don't waste it
living someone else's life. Don't be trapped
by dogma, which is living with the results of
other people's thinking. Don't let the noise of
other's opinions drown out your own inner
voice. And most importantly, have the courage
to follow your heart and intuition."
- Steve Jobs

"To choose time is to save time."
- Francis Bacon

"The unexamined life is not worth living."
- Socrates

"By swallowing evil words unsaid, no
one has ever harmed his stomach."
- Sir Winston Churchill

"Preach the Gospel at all times,
and if necessary, use words."
- St. Francis of Assisi

"If a man is called to be a street sweeper, he should
sweep streets even as Michelangelo painted, or
Beethoven composed music or Shakespeare wrote
poetry. He should sweep streets so well that all the
hosts of heaven and earth will pause to say, 'Here
lived a great street sweeper who did his job well."
- Martin Luther King Jr.

"It takes twenty years to build a reputation
and five minutes to ruin it. If you think about
that, you will do things differently."
- Warren Buffett

"Never try to walk up a wall that is leaning
towards you. Never try to kiss somebody
who is leaning away from you and NEVER
EVER try to speak to a group that knows
more about a subject than you do."
- Sir Winston Churchill

"The pebbles of knowledge must be bonded

together by the cement of experience."
- R.G. LeTourneau

"Where did you get your good judgment?"
"From my experience." "And where did you get
your experience?" "From my bad judgment."
- R.G. LeTourneau

"A day will come when the story inside
you will want to breathe on its own.
That's when you'll start writing."
- Sarah Noffke

"We don't stop laughing because we get old,
we get old because we stop laughing."
- Unknown

"The stories people tell have a way of taking
care of them. If stories come to you, care for
them. And learn to give them away where
they are needed. Sometimes a person needs
a story more than food to stay alive"
- Jean Shinoda Bolen

"The internet is the first thing that humanity
has built that humanity doesn't understand."
- Eric Schmidt

"Educating the mind without educating
the heart is not educating at all."

- Aristotle (*Attributed*)

"Those who are likely never to have any great
use or aptitude for mathematics should be
allowed to rest, more or less, upon their oars."
-Dorothy Sayers

"Go for it now. The future is promised to no one."
- Wayne Dyer

"What you have to learn to do, we learn by doing."
- Aristotle

"Cheerfulness and content are great beautifiers
and are famous preservers of youthful looks."
- Charles Dickens

"The ideals which have always shone
before me and filled me with the joy of
living are goodness, beauty, and truth."
- Albert Einstein

"It is better that joy should be spread over
all day in the form of strength than that it
should be concentrated into ecstasies..."
- Ralph Waldo Emerson

"The faintest pen is better than
the brightest brain."
- Anonymous

"Happiness is a perfume you cannot pour on
others without getting a few drops on yourself."
- Ralph Waldo Emerson

"Opportunity of a lifetime must be seized
within the lifetime of the opportunity."
- Rick Rigsby

"As soon as something stops being fun, it's time
to move on. Life is too short to be unhappy."
- Sir Richard Branson

"There is some good in this world,
and it's worth fighting for."
- J.R.R. Tolkien

"Twenty years from now you will be
more disappointed by the things that you
didn't do than by the ones you did do."
- H. Jackson Brown Jr.

"It is better to be hated for what you are
than to be loved for what you are not."
- André Gide

"Uneasy lies the head that wears a crown."
- William Shakespeare

"Every human life is worth the

same and worth saving."
- J.K. Rowling

"The goal isn't to live forever; the goal
is to create something that will."
- Chuck Palahniuk

"All endings are also beginnings. We
just don't know it at the time."
- Mitch Albom

"It's no use going back to yesterday because
I was a different person then."
- Lewis Carroll

"The only limits for tomorrow are
the doubts we have today."
- Pittacus Lore

"If we wait until we're ready, we'll be
waiting for the rest of our lives."
- Lemony Snicket

"While we are postponing, life speeds by."
- Lucius Annaeus Seneca

"Not all those who wander are lost."
- J.R.R. Tolkien

"If you're making mistakes it means

you're out there doing something."
- Neil Gaiman

"Even a stopped clock is right twice a day."
- Paulo Coelho

"So many things are possible just as long
as you don't know they're impossible."
- Norton Juster

"Get busy living or get busy dying."
- Stephen King, *Different Seasons*

"Nothing that's worthwhile is ever easy."
- Nicholas Sparks

"When you want something, all the universe
conspires in helping you to achieve it."
- Paulo Coelho

"There is nothing in the world so irresistibly
contagious as laughter and good humor."
- Charles Dickens

"The saddest people I've ever met in life are the
ones who don't care deeply about anything at
all. Passion and satisfaction go hand in hand, and
without them, any happiness is only temporary,
because there's nothing to make it last."
- Nicholas Sparks

"You can't stay in your corner of the
Forest waiting for others to come to you.
You have to go to them sometimes."
- A.A. Milne

"We can only be said to be alive in those moments
when our hearts are conscious of our treasures."
- Thornton Wilder

"It is never too late to be wise."
- Daniel Defoe

"The years teach much which
the days never knew."
- Ralph Waldo Emerson

"To live is the rarest thing in the world.
Most people exist, that is all."
- Oscar Wilde

"Laughter cleanses the soul and
refreshes the mind."
- Maggy Byrd

"Delay is preferable to error."
- Thomas Jefferson

"Humanity, take a good look at yourself. Inside,
you've got heaven and earth, and all of creation.

You are a world-everything is hidden in you."
- Hildegard of Bingen

"My concern is not whether God is on
our side; my greatest concern is to be on
God's side, for God is always right."
- Abraham Lincoln

"Try to say nothing negative about anybody
for three days, for forty-five days, for three
months. See what happens to your life."
- Yoko Ono

"It is never too late to be what
you might have been."
- George Eliot

"Character is like a tree and reputation
like its shadow. The shadow is what we
think of it; the tree is the real thing."
- Abraham Lincoln

"Let your joy be in your journey-
not in some distant goal."
- Tim Cook

"Take one day at a time. Today, after all, is the
tomorrow you worried about yesterday."
- Billy Graham

"Every book, remember, is dead until a reader
activates it by reading. Every time you read
you are walking among the dead, and, if you are
listening, you just might hear prophecies."
- Kathy Acker

"Any fool can be happy. It takes a man
with real heart to make beauty out of
the stuff that makes us weep."
- Clive Barker

"A bird doesn't sing because it has an
answer, it sings because it has a song."
- Maya Angelou

"A baby is God's opinion that life should go on."
- Carl Sandburg

"When you're at the end of your
rope, tie a knot and hold on."
- Theodore Roosevelt

"Be kind, for everyone you meet
is fighting a harder battle."
- Plato

"A time comes when you need to stop
waiting for the man you want to become and
start being the man you want to be."

- Bruce Springsteen

"I'm never more productive than at 4 a.m."
- Sallie Krawcheck

"You may shoot me with your words, You may
cut me with your eyes, You may kill me with
your hatefulness, But still, like air, I'll rise."
-Maya Angelou

"Character consists of what you do
on the third and fourth tries."
- James Mechener

"You may not control all the events
that happen to you, but you can decide
not to be reduced by them."
- Maya Angelou

"Do the best you can until you know better.
Then when you know better, do better."
- Maya Angelou

"The brave man is not he who does not feel
afraid, but he who conquers that fear."
- Nelson Mandela

"We cannot change the past, but we can change
our attitude toward it. Uproot guilt and plant
forgiveness. Tear out arrogance and seed humility.

Exchange love for hate --- thereby, making the present comfortable and the future promising."
- Maya Angelou

"If you don't like something, change it. If you can't change it, change your attitude. Don't complain."
- Maya Angelou

"A person starts to live when he can live outside himself."
- Albert Einstein

"Don't try to memorize anything that you can look up."
- Albert Einstein

"The difference between what we do and what we are capable of doing would suffice to solve most of the world's problems."
- Mahatma Gandhi

"Character is what you are in the dark."
- Dwight L. Moody

"Life's most persistent and urgent question is, 'what are we doing for others?'"
- Martin Luther King, Jr.

"To be what we are, and to become what we are

capable of becoming is the only end of life."
- Robert Louis Stevenson

"A major stimulant to creative thinking is focused questions. There is something about a well-worded question that often penetrates to the heart of the matter and triggers new ideas and insights."
- Brian Tracy

"The ideas I use are mostly the ideas of people who don't develop them."
- Thomas Edison

"Whatever the mind can conceive, it can achieve..."
- Paul Meyer

"And whatever your heart desires and you ardently pursue it, shall inevitably come to pass."
- Anonymous

"If you don't like someone's story, write your own."
- Chinua Achebe

"Jack of all trades is always a master of nothing and a rolling stone gathers no moth."
- Anonymous

"Your role, plus your goal, plus

your toil equals success."
- Robert Schuller

"It costs a lot to look cheap."
- Dolly Parton

"Lives of great men will remind us we
can make our lives sublime."
- Henry Wordsworth Longfellow

"If you are a leader, lead well; If you are an
administrator, administer well; If you are a
manager, manage well; If you are a preacher, preach
well; If you are an inspector, inspect well; If you are
a teacher, teach well; If you are a farmer, farm well;
If you are a trader, trade well; If you are a ruler, rule
well; If you are a judge, judge well; If you are a driver,
drive well; If you are a student, study well; If you
are military personnel, defend the country well."
- Professor Jerry Gana

"I can turn nothing into something, pennies
into a fortune, and disaster into triumph."
- Anonymous

"Success is simply a matter of
luck. Ask any failure."
- Earl Wilson

"The longer you postpone a thing the

less likely you are to get at it."
- Mark Twain

"Not everything that is faced can be changed,
but nothing can be changed until it is faced."
- Brandi Harless

"When I was young, I thought that
money was the most important thing in
life; now that I am old, I know it is."
- Oscar Wilde

"When it's a question of money, everybody
is of the same religion."
- Voltaire

"Virtue has never been as respectable as money."
- Mark Twain

"If you want to feel rich, just count the
things you have that money can't buy."
- Proverb

"Money without brains is always dangerous."
- Napoleon Hill

"I've missed more than 9000 shots in my
career. I've lost almost 300 games. 26 times I've
been trusted to take the game-winning shot
and missed. I've failed over and over and over

again in my life. And that is why I succeed."
- Michael Jordan

"Work like there is someone working 24
hours a day to take it away from you."
- Mark Cuban

"By perseverance, the snail reached the ark."
- Charles Spurgeon

"Spread love everywhere you go: First of
all, in your own house. Give love to your
children, to your wife or husband, to a next-
door neighbor…Let no one ever come to you
without leaving better and happier. Be the
living expression of God's kindness; kindness
in your face, kindness in your eyes, kindness in
your smile, kindness in your warm greeting."
- Mother Teresa

"It's not how much we do – it's how
much love we put into the doing."
- Mother Teresa

"Most humans are never fully present in the
now because unconsciously they believe that the
next moment must be more important than this
one. But then you miss your whole life, which is
never not now. And that's a revelation for some
people. To realize that your life is only ever now."

- Eckhart Tolle

"I'd rather be a corpse than a coward."
- Mary Ellen Pleasant

"One of the illusions of life is that the
present hour is not the critical, decisive
hour. Write it on your heart that every
day is the best day of the year."
- Ralph Waldo Emerson

"People say we shouldn't laugh in church.
What good father will not want to hear
his children's laughter in his house."
- Michael Jr., *Comedian*

"If you allow a hypocrite to come between
you and God, the hypocrite is actually
closer to God than you are."
- Zig Ziglar

"Focus on your feet, not your head.
Keep them moving forward."
- Jen Welter, *the first woman to coach in the NFL*

"One kind word can warm three winter months."
- Japanese Proverb

"Four things come not back-the spoken
word, the sped arrow, the past life, and

the neglected opportunity."
- Arabian Proverb

"God will never appear to a hungry
man except in the form of bread."
- Mahatma Gandhi

"Every day I put hope on the line. I don't
know one thing about the future. I don't
know what the next hour will hold."
- Eugene Peterson

"The most powerful tool most of
us possess is our own voice."
- Joyce Maynard

"The greatest and kindest gift we can
give to our loved ones is that we continue
to work on ourselves."
- Williamson

"I use a book as a tool to grow myself bigger
and I lend them away to help other people."
- Ely Perry

"I want my children to be surrounded with
the best things ever written. Maybe some
of it will lodge in their minds and stay with
them always to add to their lives."
- Anna Peale, *the mother of Norman Vincent Peale*

"Carry out a random act of kindness, with no
expectation of reward, safe in the knowledge that
one day someone might do the same for you."
- Princess Diana

"A child cannot pay for its mother's milk."
- Chinua Achebe

"If you want peace, work for justice."
- Pope Paul VI

"If we could untangle the mysteries of life and
unravel the energies which run through the world;
if we could evaluate correctly the significance
of passing events; if we could measure the
struggles, dilemmas, and aspirations of mankind,
we could find that nothing is born out of time
Everything comes at its appointed moment."
- Joseph R. Sizoo

"Science without religion is lame. Religion
without science is blind."
- Albert Einstein

"A person who never made a mistake
never tried anything new."
- Albert Einstein

"This above all: to thine own self be true,

and it must follow, as the night the day, thou
'canst not then be false to any man."
- William Shakespeare

"Service to others is the rent you pay
for your room here on earth."
- Mohammed Ali

"I think age is just something that is a number,
and it depends on whether the number is
going to keep you down or keep you up."
- Irwin Winkler, *producer of the movie, Rocky*

"Simplicity is the ultimate sophistication."
- Leonard Da Vinci

"Do things for people not because of
who they are or what they do in return.
But because of who you are."
- Harold S. Kushner

"Learn from yesterday, live for today,
hope for tomorrow. The important
thing is not to stop questioning."
- Albert Einstein

"One of the truest tests of integrity is its
blunt refusal to be compromised."
- Chinua Achebe

"You become. It takes a long time. That's why
it doesn't often happen to people who break
easily, or have sharp edges, or who have to be
carefully kept. Generally, by the time you are
Real, most of your hair has been loved off, and
your eyes drop out and you get loose in the joints
and very shabby. But these things don't matter
at all, because once you are Real you can't be
ugly, except to people who don't understand."
- Margery Williams

"Love is the extremely difficult realization
that something other than oneself is real."
- Iris Murdoch

"True friendship multiplies the good in life
and divides its evils. Strive to have friends,
for life without friends is like life on a desert
island....to find one real friend in a lifetime is
good fortune, to keep him is a blessing."
- Baltasar Gracian

"Few are those who see with their own
eyes and feel with their own hearts."
- Albert Einstein

"Books and all forms of writing are terror
to those who wish to suppress the truth."
- Wole Soyinka

"Everyone should be respected as an
individual, but no one idolized."
- Albert Einstein

"Never play with the feelings of others, because
you may win the game, but the risk is that you
will surely lose the person for a lifetime."
- William Shakespeare

"The world suffers a lot. Not because of
the violence of bad people, But because
of the silence of good people!"
- Napoleon Bonaparte

"When you are in light, everything will
follow you. But you enter dark, even your
own shadow will not follow you!"
- Adolf Hitler

"Imagination is everything. It is the
preview of life's coming attractions."
- Albert Einstein

"If you can't explain it simply, you
don't understand it well enough."
- Albert Einstein

"Be the change you wish to see in the world."
- Mahatma Gandhi

"Every gardener knows that under the cloak of
winter lies a miracle...a seed waiting to sprout, a
bulb opening to the light, a bud straining to unfurl.
And the anticipation nurtures our dream."
- Barbara Winkler

"Lead me from the unreal to the Real; from
darkness to Light; from death to immortality."
- Upanishads

"I will love the light for it shows me
the way, yet I will endure the darkness
because it shows me the stars."
- Og Mandino

"There are two ways of spreading light: To
be the candle or the mirror that reflects it."
- Edith Wharton

"How does one become a butterfly?" she asked
pensively. "You must want to fly so much that
you are willing to give up being a caterpillar."
- Trina Paulus

"Do not be embarrassed by your failures,
learn from them, and start again."
- Sir Richard Branson

"It's fine to celebrate success but it is more

important to heed the lessons of failure."
- Bill Gates

"I can honestly say that I have never gone
into any business purely to make money.
If that is the sole motive, then I believe
you are better off doing nothing."
- Sir Richard Branson

"Distance tests a horse's strength. Time
reveals a person's character."
- Chinese Proverb

"Everything has beauty, but not everyone sees it."
- Confucius

"A single conversation with a wise man
is worth a month's study of books."
- Chinese Proverb

"Honesty is a very expensive gift don't
expect it from cheap people."
- Warren Buffett

"If you survived a storm, you won't
be bothered by the rain."
- Chinese Proverb

"You can't go back and change the beginning, but
you can start where you are and change the ending."

- C.S. Lewis

"Only a fool tests the depth of
a river with both feet."
- African Proverb

"If your mind is strong, all difficult things
will become easy. If your mind is weak, all
easy things will become difficult."
- Chinese Proverb

"Those who accomplish great things
pay attention to little ones."
- African Proverb

"We are twice armed if we fight with faith."
- Plato

"I'm not a businessman, I'm a business, man."
- Jay Z

"He will win who knows when to
fight and when not to fight."
- Chinese Proverb

"There is risk in every business, if you are not
brave enough to grab on the first or next opportunities then you shall be a poor person forever."
- Robert Kuok

"If you want to go quickly, go alone. If
you want to go far, go together."
- African Proverb

"Art is never finished, only abandoned."
- Leonard Da Vinci

"Tears come from the heart and
not from the brain."
- Leonard Da Vinci

"Wise men speak because they have something
to say; Fools because they have to say something."
- Plato

"Take rest; a field that has rested
gives a bountiful crop."
- Ovid

"I do not see disabilities, but *different* abilities."
- Rachel Hollis

"Any people that is starved with books, especially
the right type of books, will suffer intellectual
malnutrition, stagnation and atrophy."
- Obafemi Awolowo

"No matter how old an individual may be,
no matter if he is young or old, if he thinks in
accordance with the times, he is immortal."

- Nnamdi Azikiwe

"Let us not take ourselves too seriously.
None of us has a monopoly on wisdom."
- Queen Elizabeth II

"There are two things a person should
never be angry at, what they can
help, and what they cannot."
- Plato

"In this world, nothing can be said to be
certain, except death and taxes."
- Benjamin Franklin

"There is no harm in repeating a good thing."
- Plato

"The man who does things makes many
mistakes, but he never makes the biggest
mistake of all-doing nothing."
- Benjamin Franklin

"You may delay, but time will not."
- Benjamin Franklin

"The greatest wealth is to live content
with little."
- Plato

"Three may keep a secret if two of them are dead."
- Benjamin Franklin

"It's all to do with the training: you can
do a lot if you're properly trained."
- Queen Elizabeth II

"The most important thing is to improve yourself
and give it your best. Then many things previously
thought to be impossible will become possible."
- Li Ka Shing

"He that is of the opinion money will
do everything may well be suspected
of doing everything for money."
- Benjamin Franklin

"It takes many good deeds to build a good
reputation, and only one bad to lose it."
- Benjamin Franklin

"Those who make the worst use of their time
are the first to complain of its brevity."
- Jean de La Bruyère

"Time takes it all, whether you want it to or not."
- Stephen King

"Formula for handling people: Listen to the other

person's story; Listen to the other person's *full* story; Listen to the other person's story *first*."
- General George Marshall

"Wine is constant proof that God loves us and loves to see us happy."
- Benjamin Franklin

"It takes tremendous discipline to control the influence, the power you have over other people's lives."
- Clint Eastwood

"A man who dares to waste one hour of time has not discovered the value of life."
- Charles Darwin

"As if you could kill time without injuring eternity."
- Henry David Thoreau

"Aerodynamically, the bumblebee shouldn't be able to fly, but the bumblebee doesn't know it, so it goes on flying anyway."
- Mary Kay Ash

"We all boil at different degrees."
- Clint Eastwood

"Cowards falter, but danger is often

overcome by those who nobly dare."
- Queen Elizabeth II

"Start by doing what's necessary;
then do what's possible; and suddenly
you are doing the impossible."
- Francis of Assisi

"Opportunity lies in the place
where the complaints are."
- Jack Ma

"Do not wait until the conditions are perfect to
begin. Beginning makes the conditions perfect."
- Alan Cohen

"I never went to a university, and I am proud to
say so because I don't think I have done too badly."
- Folorunsho Alakija, *the richest
black woman in the world*

"You cannot show people only the petals
and not the thorns. It's not fair to them."
- Bethenny Frankel

"The closest distance between two
people is a good laugh."
- Victor Borge

"You know children are growing up when they

start asking questions that have answers."
- John Plomp

"Marriage is the alliance of two people,
one of whom never remembers birthdays
and the other who never forgets."
- Ogden Nash

"Cleaning your house while your kids
are still growing is like shoveling the
walk before it stops snowing."
- Phyllis Diller

"There is a loftier ambition than merely
to stand high in the world. It is to stoop
down and lift mankind a little higher."
- Henry Van Dyke

"If you don't think every day is a
good day, just try missing one."
- Cavett Robert

"How vain it is to sit down and write
when you have not stood up to live."
- Thoreau

"If a man does not make new acquittances
as he advances through life, he will soon
find himself left alone. A man should keep
his friendship in a constant repair."

- Samuel Johnson

"The little things? The little moments?
They aren't little."
- John Kabat-Zinn

"The difficulty lies not so much in developing
new ideas as in escaping from old ones."
- John Maynard Keynes

"An eye for eye only ends up making
the whole world blind."
- Mohandas Gandhi

"Don't assume a door is closed, push on
it. Do not assume if it was closed yesterday
that it is closed today."
- Marian Wright Edelman

"It is by going into the abyss that we recover
the treasures of life. Where you stumble,
there lies your treasure."
- Joseph Campbell

"Careers, like rockets, don't always take off on
schedule. The key is to keep working the engines."
- Gary Sinise

"Do one thing every day that scares you."
- Eleanor Roosevelt

"It takes nothing to join the crowd. It
takes everything to stand alone."
- Hans F. Hansen

"Inspiration exists, but it must find you working."
- Pablo Picasso

"Nothing is a waste of time if you
use the experience wisely."
- Auguste Rodin

"If you cannot do great things, do
small things in a great way."
- Margaret Thatcher

"The world is more malleable than you think
and it's waiting for you to hammer it into shape."
- Bono

"Courage is the first of human qualities because
it is the quality which guarantees the others."
- Aristotle

"You can't change the cards life has dealt you,
but you can determine the way you'll play them."
- Ty Boyd

"We have to get comfortable with discomfort
because we will experience it frequently

when we seek to change the status quo."
- Quint Studer

"There are three things extremely hard:
steel, a diamond, and to know one's self."
- Benjamin Franklin

"We don't count a man's years until he
has nothing else left to count."
- Ralph Waldo Emerson

"Don't be critical of your mate's faults.
It was those very defects that kept him
or her from getting a better mate."
- Zig Ziglar

"A hundred times every day I remind myself
that my inner and outer life are based on
the labors of other men living and dead, and
that I must exert myself in order to give in
the same measure as I have received."
- Albert Einstein

"Sometimes you have to go with your heart
and seize the opportunity when a door opens-
even if security doesn't seem to be apparent."
- Emmit Fox

"Two sure ways to fail: Think and
never fail or do and never think."

- Zig Ziglar

"A mistake: An event, the full benefit of which
has not yet been turned to your advantage."
- Edward Land

"The dictionary is the only place that success
comes before work. Hard work is the price we
must pay for success. I think you can accomplish
almost anything if you're willing to pay the price."
- Vince Lombardi

"Do you love life? Then do not squander
time, for that's the stuff life is made of."
- Benjamin Franklin

"Some people are so poor, all they have is money."
- Bob Marley

"There is nothing more powerful than
an idea whose time has come."
- Victor Hugo

"It's a poor sort of memory that only works
backward. Life isn't lived in reverse, yet many
people focus more time and energy on the past
than on the memories they can create today. Take
initiative by doing fun activities, starting new
traditions, and scheduling time together. Don't let
time just pass without making the most of it."

- Lewis Carroll

"Almost anything you do today will be forgotten in just a few weeks. The ability to retrieve a memory decreases exponentially unless boosted by artificial aids such as diaries and photographs. Take pictures, write in a journal, and buy souvenirs so that you have keepsakes to keep the memory alive. These physical reminders evoke the emotions of pleasant times spent with friends and family. Don't miss the opportunity to make significant memories with those you love. Jobs and experiences come and go, but shared memories last a lifetime. They keep us connected in a special way. Take advantage of that blessing every day."
- John McCrone

"A mistake: An event, the full benefit of which has not yet been turned to your advantage."
- Edward Land

"I don't think you know [how much] you did [for me]. You had my brother when you were 18 years old. Three years later I came out. The odds were stacked against us; a single parent with two boys by the time you were 21 years old. Everyone told us we weren't supposed to be here [but]...you made us believe. You kept us off the streets. You kept clothes on our backs and food on the table. When you didn't eat; you made sure we ate and went to sleep

hungry. You sacrificed for us. You're the real MVP."
- Kevin Durant

"I have a dream that my four children will
one day live in a nation where they will
not be judged by the color of their skin, but
by the content of their character."
- Martin Luther King Jr.

"Almost anything you do today will be forgotten
in just a few weeks. Forgive yourself for your
faults and your mistakes and move on."
- Les Brown

"Be brave enough to take off the masks you wear
out there and get to know who you are underneath.
Be vulnerable enough to accept your flaws and
know they are what make you real. Be confident
enough to accept and cherish your strengths. Don't
minimize them or hide them...They are your
beautiful gifts to share with the world. Be brave
enough to say, you know what, all of this is who
I am. I make so many mistakes. I can be forgetful,
I am messy. But...I am doing my best with what
I've got. And I am so proud of that. I am so proud
of me. And I am proud of who becoming."
- Nikki Banas

"Each one of us is more than the
worst thing we've ever done."

- Sheryl Sandberg

"If you are not diligent, you may end
up leading an indigent life."
- Samson King

"You must never be fearful about what
you are doing when it is right."
- Rosa Parks

"Until the sun falls from the sky, we will
have enough light to bask in and to share."
- Harris Faulkner

"Advice is like kissing, it costs nothing
and it's a pleasant thing to do."
- George Bernard Shaw

"God gave you a gift of 84,600 seconds today.
Have you used one of them to say thank you?"
- William Arthur Ward

"Sickness comes on horseback
but departs on foot."
- Dutch Proverb

"You lose out on 100% of the opportunities
that you never go after."
- Robin Ryan

"Colors fade, temples crumble, empires
fall, but wise words endure."
- Edward Thorndike

"You cannot do a kindness too soon for you
never know how soon it will be too late."
- Ralph Waldo Emerson

"Life is a succession of lessons which
must be lived to be understood."
- Ralph Waldo Emerson

"A person without a sense of humor is
like a wagon without springs. It's jolted
by every pebble on the road."
- Henry Ward Beecher

"Imagine life as a game in which you are juggling
five balls in the air. You name them – work, family,
health, friends, and spirit – and you're keeping
all of these in the air. You will soon understand
that work is a rubber ball. If you drop it, it will
bounce back. But the other four balls – family,
health, friends, and spirit – are made of glass. If
you drop one of these, they will be irrevocably
scuffed, marked, nicked, damaged, or even
shattered. They will never be the same."
- Brian Dyson

"As soap is to the body, so laughter is to the soul."
- Jewish Proverb

"Be who you are and say what you feel,
because those who mind don't matter
and those who matter don't mind."
- Dr. Seuss

"Don't watch the clock; do what
it does. Keep going."
- Sam Levenson

"Tell me and I'll forget; show me and I may
remember; involve me and I'll understand."
- Chinese Proverb

"Don't let your failures define
you – let them teach you."
- Barack Obama

"Learn everything you can, anytime you can,
from anyone you can – there will always come
a time when you will be grateful you did."
- Sarah Caldwell

"When you come to a roadblock, take a detour."
- Mary Kay Ash

"A lot of leaders fail because they don't have the

bravery to touch that nerve or strike that chord."
- Kobe Bryant

"It is better to be prepared for an opportunity
and not have one, than to have an opportunity
and not be prepared."
- Whitney Young

"How far you go in life depends on your being
tender with the young, compassionate with the
aged, sympathetic with the striving and tolerant
of the weak and strong. Because someday in
your life you will have been all of these."
- George Washington Carver

"It is the one thing you can control. You
are responsible for how people remember
you—or don't. So, don't take it lightly."
- Kobe Bryant

"The least movement is of importance to all
nature. The entire ocean is affected by a pebble."
- Blaise Pascal

"My parents are my backbone. Still are.
They're the only group that will support
you if you score zero or you score 40."
- Kobe Bryant

NUGGETS FROM ENTREPRENEURS

Ray Kroc, Dave Thomas, Colonel Sanders, Samuel Truett Cathy, Booker T. Washington, Bill Gates, Oprah Winfrey, Sam Walton, Chris Gardner

Ray Kroc, *McDonald's*

"As long as you're green, you're growing.
As soon as you're ripe, you start to rot."

"Take calculated risks. Act boldly and
thoughtfully. Be an agile company."

"If you're not a risk-taker, you should
get the hell out of business."

"The quality of a leader is reflected in the
standards they set for themselves."

"It's easy to have principles when
you're rich. The important thing is to
have principles when you're poor."

"I have always believed that each man makes
his own happiness and is responsible for his
own problems. It is a simple philosophy."

"Adversity can strengthen you if you
have the will to grind it out."

"It is no achievement to walk a tightrope
laid flat on the floor."

"I refused to worry about more than one
thing at a time, and I would not let useless
fretting about a problem, no matter how
important, keep me from sleeping."

Dave Thomas, *Wendy's Founder*

"Honesty and integrity are the foundation upon which every successful person stands. Dishonest people don't make it in the long run. Throughout your life, you'll have the opportunity to cut corners and take some short cuts. Don't do it! If you lose your integrity, you've lost everything you set out to gain. Earn and appreciate the trust of the people you work with and respect. You earn your reputation by the things you do every day. And at the end of the day, all a man has is his integrity."

"Hard work is good for the soul, and it keeps you from feeling sorry for yourself because you don't have time."

"Don't be afraid to be unique or speak your mind, because that's what makes you different from everyone else."

"Get all the education you can. Who knows what more I could have achieved if I'd stayed in school and went to college? The possibilities are endless when you have an education."

"Share your success and help others succeed. Give everyone a chance to have a piece of the pie. If the pie's not big enough, make a bigger pie."

Colonel Sanders, *KFC*

"I've only had two rules. Do all you can and do it the best you can. It's the only way you ever get that feeling of accomplishing something."

"The easy way is efficacious and speedy, the hard way arduous and long. But, as the clock ticks, the easy way becomes harder and the hard way becomes easier. And as the calendar records the years, it becomes increasingly evident that the easy way rests hazardously upon shifting sands, whereas the hard way builds solidly a foundation of confidence that cannot be swept away."

"Hard work beats all the tonics and vitamins in the world."

"There's no reason to be the richest man in the cemetery. You can't do any business from there."

"Wealth, like happiness, is never attained when sought after directly. It comes as a byproduct of providing a useful service."

Samuel Truett Cathy, *Chick-fil-A*

"If you wish to enrich days, plant flowers; If you
wish to enrich years, plant trees; If you wish to
enrich Eternity, plant ideals in the lives of others."

"I enjoy few things more than making
people – especially children – smile."

"We live in a changing world, but we need to
be reminded that the important things have
not changed, and the important things will not
change if we keep our priorities in proper order."

"Wealth has the power to build
up and to destroy."

"Our sweetest memories are
often simpler times…"

"When we share our time with children, the little
things often become lifetime memories for them."

"The unexpected opportunity I enjoy most is
the opportunity to turn a frown into a smile."

"As I read Mr. Hill's book, I realized I could
do anything if I wanted it badly enough.
His words motivated me and showed me
that I live in a do-it-yourself world."

SAMSON OLUSANYA KING

*[On reading Napoleon Hill's 'Think and Grow
Rich' book as a high school student]*

Booker T. Washington

"You can't hold a man down without
staying down with him."

"Associate yourself with people of
good quality, for it is better to be alone
than to be in bad company."

"No race can prosper till it learns that there is as
much dignity in tilling a field as in writing a poem."

"The older I grow, the more I am convinced
that there is no education which one can
get from books and costly apparatus that
is equal to that which can be gotten from
contact with great men and women."

"If you want to lift yourself up,
lift up someone else."

"Success always leaves footprints."

"Egotism is the anesthetic that
dulls the pain of stupidity."

"There is no power on earth that can neutralize
the influence of a high, simple and useful life."

"The happiest people are those who do

the most for others. The most miserable
are those who do the least."

Bill Gates, *Microsoft*

"It's fine to celebrate success, but it is more important to heed the lessons of failure."

"Life is not divided into semesters. You don't get summers off, and very few employers are interested in helping you. Find yourself."

"Whether I'm at the office, at home, or on the road, I always have a stack of books I'm looking forward to reading."

"Don't compare yourself with anyone in this world, if you do so, you are insulting yourself."

"I failed in some subjects in exam, but my friend passed in all. Now he is an engineer in Microsoft and I am the owner of Microsoft."

"People always fear change. People feared electricity when it was invented, didn't they?"

"I really had a lot of dreams when I was a kid, and I think a great deal of that grew out of the fact that I had a chance to read a lot."

Oprah Winfrey, *media mogul*

"When you undervalue what you do, the
world will undervalue who you are."

"Be thankful for what you have; you'll end up
having more. If you concentrate on what you
don't have, you will never, ever have enough."

"Real integrity is doing the right thing,
knowing that nobody's going to know
whether you did it or not."

"One of the hardest things in life to learn are
which bridges to cross and which bridges to burn."

"Challenges are gifts that force us to
search for a new center of gravity. Don't fight
them. Just find a new way to stand."
"The thing you fear most has no power.
Your fear of it is what has the power. Facing
the truth really will set you free."

"Surround yourself only with people
who are going to take you higher."

"Think like a queen. A queen is not afraid to fail.
Failure is another steppingstone to greatness."

"You get in life what you have the courage

to ask for."

"The key to realizing a dream is to focus
not on success but on significance — and then
even the small steps and little victories along
your path will take on greater meaning."

"I was raised to believe that excellence
is the best deterrent to racism and sexism
and that's how I operate my life."

Sam Walton, *Walmart*

"There is only one boss. The customer.
And he can fire everybody in the company
from the chairman on down, simply by
spending his money somewhere else."

"Celebrate your successes. Find
some humor in your failures."

"Most of us don't invent ideas. We take
the best ideas from someone else."

"Keep everybody guessing as to what your next
trick is going to be. Don't become too predictable."

"Nothing else can quite substitute for a few
well-chosen, well-timed, sincere words of praise.
They're absolutely free and worth a fortune."

"To succeed in this world, you have
to change all the time."

"Ignore the conventional wisdom. If
everybody else is doing it one way, there's
a good chance you can find your niche by
going in exactly the opposite direction."

Chris Gardner

"The secret to success: find something
you love to do so much, you can't wait for
the sun to rise to do it all over again."

"I was late once, and it cost me $50,000. I
figure it was cheaper to wear two watches."

"The balance in your life is more important
than the balance in your checking account."

"The world is your oyster. It's up
to you to find the pearls."

"I was homeless, but I wasn't hopeless.
I knew a better day was coming."

" Wealth can also be that attitude of
gratitude with which we remind ourselves
every day to count our blessings."

FINAL THOUGHT

Let us be real, we all go through those moments when it seems we are not motivated or inspired because motivation is elusive. Some days it is like you are going through the motions and you are tempted to quit, give up or throw in the towel. At such a moment, I encourage you to take a deep breath and go through some of these inspirational quotes and you will discover that words are conveyors of energy. You will be inspired and energized with a fresh passion to face life. In the words of Dr. Robert Schuller, "Tough times don't last but tough people do."

Remember, no matter what battle or challenge you are facing in life right now, YOU ARE NEVER ALONE!

ACKNOWLEDGEMENT

It is very difficult to give full and adequate recognition to all those whose thoughts, life stories, and words have touched my life in one way or another, but I must acknowledge the immense contribution of a handful of individuals, as friends, mentors, and colleagues without mentioning names because they know themselves. You all remain the rock of my heritage.

To the numerous men and women whose words have inspired me greatly to pursue excellence each day for a greater purpose. I am especially grateful to all my readers for your constant love and support. Thank You!

To my lovely children – Blessing, Faith, Faith Tolani (goddaughter), and Isaac, I am grateful for the privilege of having you in my life. And to my Lump of Delight, Precious Oludolapo Ibilola Apeke, you are the real MVP in my world, and I am grateful to be doing life with you!

ABOUT THE AUTHOR

Samson Olusanya King

Samson King is a man with an uncommon passion for humanity, irrespective of class, race, color, continent, and differences. Since relocated to the United States from Africa, he has worked with Fortune 500 company, organized seminars, and workshops on various topics for participants from within and outside of the United States, and as well served in different capacities for non-profit organizations.

Samson currently provides spiritual and pastoral care to patients, families, and staff at Miami Valley Hospital, Dayton, and Mount Carmel Health Systems as a Chaplain, both in Ohio. He also teaches World Religions at Felbry College School of Nursing in Columbus Ohio. Samson has degrees in Engineering, Education, and Theology, respectively.

Samson met his college sweetheart, Oludolapo Precious, for the first time in 1994, and they have been married for nearly two decades. They both reside in

Columbus Ohio, where they raise their lovely children.

PRAISE FOR AUTHOR

Before You Go!

I would like to thank you for buying this book. I know you could have picked from hundreds of quotation books, but you took a chance with me. Can I ask you a huge favor? Please take a minute to to online and leave a review on Amazon for this book.

Reviews are the single biggest gift you can give to authors because they are tough to get but count for so much. Thank You!

SAMSON KING, B.E.E, M.Div.
sam1king@outlook.com

BOOKS BY THIS AUTHOR

Unstuck: Don't Let Your Stories And Uniqueness Die With You! 7 Reasons You Should Publish Your Book Now!

In The Company Of The Greats

A Biblical Posture That Changed My Life

How To Be Led By The Holy Spirit

An Exemplar Of Kindness

Commanding Supernatural Results Straight From The Holy Bible

www.ingramcontent.com/pod-product-compliance
Lightning Source LLC
Chambersburg PA
CBHW072029150726